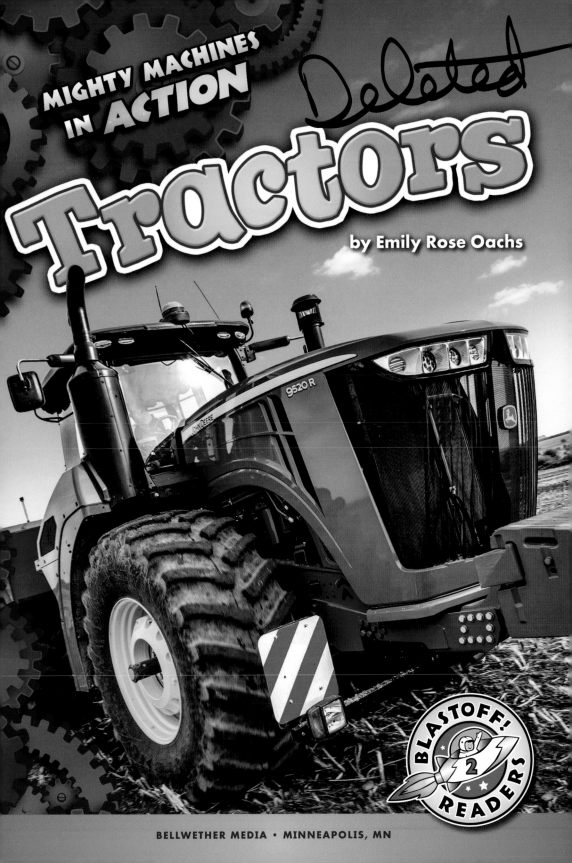

MIGHTY MACHINES IN ACTION

Deleted

Tractors

by Emily Rose Oachs

9520 R

JOHN DEERE

BLASTOFF! READERS 2

BELLWETHER MEDIA • MINNEAPOLIS, MN

Note to Librarians, Teachers, and Parents:

Blastoff! Readers are carefully developed by literacy experts and combine standards-based content with developmentally appropriate text.

Level 1 provides the most support through repetition of high-frequency words, light text, predictable sentence patterns, and strong visual support.

Level 2 offers early readers a bit more challenge through varied simple sentences, increased text load, and less repetition of high-frequency words.

Level 3 advances early-fluent readers toward fluency through increased text and concept load, less reliance on visuals, longer sentences, and more literary language.

Level 4 builds reading stamina by providing more text per page, increased use of punctuation, greater variation in sentence patterns, and increasingly challenging vocabulary.

Level 5 encourages children to move from "learning to read" to "reading to learn" by providing even more text, varied writing styles, and less familiar topics.

Whichever book is right for your reader, Blastoff! Readers are the perfect books to build confidence and encourage a love of reading that will last a lifetime!

This edition first published in 2017 by Bellwether Media, Inc.

No part of this publication may be reproduced in whole or in part without written permission of the publisher. For information regarding permission, write to Bellwether Media, Inc., Attention: Permissions Department, 5357 Penn Avenue South, Minneapolis, MN 55419.

Library of Congress Cataloging-in-Publication Data

Names: Oachs, Emily Rose, author.
Title: Tractors / by Emily Rose Oachs.
Description: Minneapolis, MN : Bellwether Media, Inc., 2017. | Series: Blastoff! Readers. Mighty Machines in Action | Audience: Ages 5-8. | Audience: K to grade 3. | Includes bibliographical references and index.
Identifiers: LCCN 2016034723 (print) | LCCN 2016035187 (ebook) | ISBN 9781626176096 (hardcover : alk. paper) | ISBN 9781681033396 (ebook)
Subjects: LCSH: Tractors–Juvenile literature.
Classification: LCC TL233.15 .O23 2017 (print) | LCC TL233.15 (ebook) | DDC 631.3/72–dc23
LC record available at https://lccn.loc.gov/2016034723

Editor: Christina Leighton   Designer: Steve Porter

Printed in the United States of America, North Mankato, MN.

Table of **Contents**

Field Machines   4

Farm Helpers   8

Implements and Engines   12

Strong and Steady   18

Glossary   22

To Learn More   23

Index   24

FIELD MACHINES

A tractor slowly moves across a field. It pulls a **baler** behind it.

baler

The field is covered in cut hay.
As the tractor drives, the baler
gathers the hay.

hay bale

Soon, the tractor brakes and the baler opens. Out drops a hay **bale**. Thud!

Then the tractor drives ahead
to make another bale!

Tractors are strong machines used for pulling heavy loads.

Farmers use them for many jobs. Without tractors, a farmer's work would be much harder!

THE LARGEST TRACTOR

Big Bud 747

height: 14 feet (4.3 meters)

average human

length: 27 feet (8.2 meters)

Farmers **plow** fields and plant seeds with tractors.

MACHINE PROFILE
JOHN DEERE 6930

length: 15.7 feet (4.8 meters)
height: 9.5 feet (2.9 meters)
power: 161 horsepower (122 kilowatts)

harvesting crops

Tractors can also help spray for pests. In the fall, tractors help **harvest** crops.

IMPLEMENTS AND ENGINES

Tractors pull **implements** behind them. Implements help tractors plow, plant, and do other work.

planter implement

drawbar

Drawbars connect implements to the tractors.

Tractors are powered by **diesel engines**. The engines can also power different implements.

diesel engine

power take-off

Spinning poles called
power take-offs (PTOs)
carry power to the implements.

Many tractors have big back tires.

They allow the tractor to drive over soft soil and mud.

Drivers control tractors from the **cab**. Many cabs have computers that map out fields.

Some computers
guide tractors
without drivers!

IDENTIFY A
TRACTOR

cab

diesel
engine

big tires

Tractors crawl down roads and across fields. They are strong and steady.

Whatever the job is, they
get it done!

Glossary

bale—a bundle of hay or straw

baler—a farm machine that collects hay or straw and binds it into bales

cab—the part of the tractor where the driver sits

diesel engines—loud engines that burn diesel fuel and are often used in big machines

drawbars—arms that connect tractors to implements

harvest—to gather crops

implements—tools that have certain tasks and are often attached to tractors

plow—to break up and turn over soil

power take-offs—spinning rods that bring energy to implements from the tractors' engines

To Learn More

AT THE LIBRARY

Dufek, Holly. *Big Tractors: With Casey & Friends.* Austin, Tex. Octane Press, 2015.

Gunzi, Christiane, and Louise Pritchard. *Mega Tractors*. Hauppauge, N.Y.: Barron's Educational Series, Inc., 2016.

Rogers, Hal. *Tractors*. Mankato, Minn.: Child's World, 2014.

ON THE WEB

Learning more about tractors is as easy as 1, 2, 3.

1. Go to www.factsurfer.com.

2. Enter "tractors" into the search box.

3. Click the "Surf" button and you will see a list of related web sites.

With factsurfer.com, finding more information is just a click away.

Index

baler, 4, 5, 6
cab, 18, 19
computers, 18, 19
crops, 11
drawbars, 13
drivers, 18, 19
drives, 5, 7, 17
engines, 14, 19
farmers, 9, 10
field, 4, 5, 10, 18, 20
harvest, 11
hay, 5, 6
implements, 12, 13, 14, 15
loads, 8
pests, 11
plant, 10, 12

plow, 10, 12
power, 10, 14, 15
power take-offs, 15
pulls, 4, 8, 12
roads, 20
size, 9, 10
spray, 11
tires, 16, 19

The images in this book are reproduced through the courtesy of: John Deere, front cover, pp. 4, 4-5, 6-7, 10-11; smereka, pp. 8-9, 13, 20-21; VRstudio, p. 10; Evgeniy Zakharov, pp. 12-13; Stanislaw Tokarski, p. 14; nulinukas, pp. 14-15; Photobac, p. 16; Chris Baker, pp. 16-17; Stocktributor, pp. 18-19; s_oleg, p. 19 (tractor); budabar, p. 19 (engine).

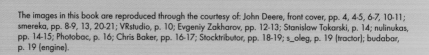